March 2002
Banff, Canada.

To our dearest
Christopher & Nicola.

We share in your joy!
May our LORD bless you
abundantly in your marriage.
It was wonderful to see you here!
all our ♡.
4 Steyns.

CANADIAN ROCKIES

Text by
CARL BENN

Photos by
Andrea Pistolesi

BONECHI

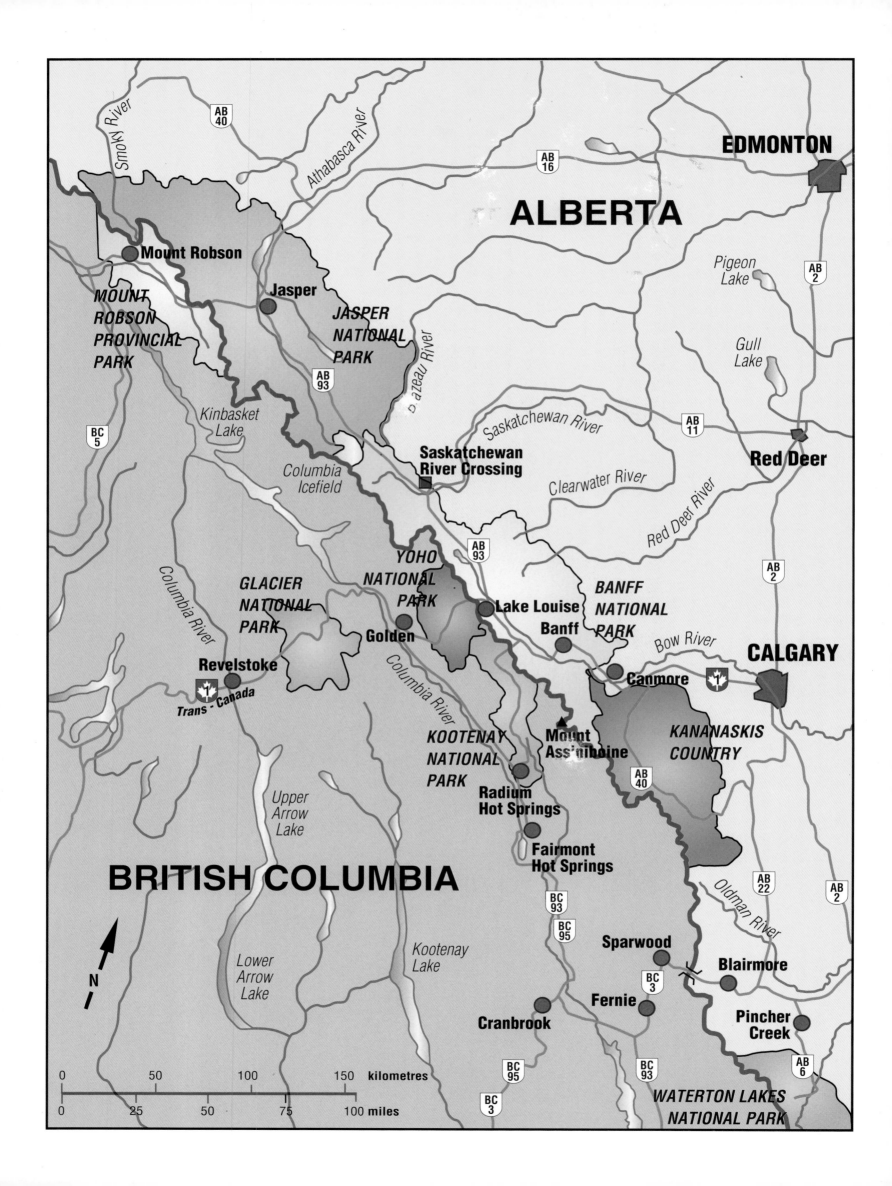

CONTENTS

INTRODUCTION

The magnificent Canadian Rockies are one of the world's most popular tourist attractions – and for good reason: they comprise some of the most glorious wilderness lands on earth, yet they also are among the most accessible natural environments on the planet. At the same time, the very best in tourism facilities sit readily at hand to cater to a traveller's every need. Alternatively, those who feel like roughing it can find challenging opportunities to experience mountain and ice climbing, white water rafting, hiking, skiing, and camping in the wild – all within a short distance of the comforts of civilization.

In 1871, British Columbia joined the Canadian Confederation, in part because of a promise that a railway would be built to connect it to central Canada. In 1883, the celebrated Canadian Pacific reached Banff, Alberta from the east. Work continued for another two years, and in 1885 the last spike of the transcontinental railway was driven into the ground at Craigellachie in the Eagle Pass of B.C. Afterwards large numbers of settlers, miners, and lumbermen moved west (sadly pushing aside most of the old native and fur trade community) in a grand quest to create the modern society that now is home to several million people in British Columbia and Alberta.

Tourism had its birth at the same time as the railways arrived. Railway companies wanted to fill the trains that travelled to and from the west, and saw tourism as part of the answer. In the 1880s, 'alpinism' gripped the imagination of middle and upper class people who wished to commune with nature amidst the rugged and sublime beauty of the world's great mountain ranges. As well, these tourists hoped to restore their bodies and wash away their stresses in the restorative hot springs that abound in the Rockies. The railways accordingly built hotels, hired guides, and provided other services to cater to these early visitors. At the same time, the Canadian government recognized that portions of the Rockies should be set aside for the public good, giving rise to the country's first national parks which grew along with provincial parks to preserve so much of the natural beauty of this magnificent region.

At this point in our story, we invite you to join us on a journey through the Canadian Rocky Mountains and enjoy the wonderful photographs on the pages below as you explore this fascinating part of the world.

BANFF NATIONAL PARK

Established in 1885, Banff National Park in Alberta is Canada's oldest national park. In 1883 railway workers explored a cave that local natives used to cure their ailments. They discovered sulphurous hot springs that had

13

commercial value in an age when 'taking the waters' was a fashionable treatment for whatever ailed people. Within a year several small enterprises opened for tourists who wanted to enjoy the springs. However, arguments arose over who owned Banff's resources, so the government created a park around the springs that has grown to encompass 6641 square kilometres of some of Canada's most breathtaking landscapes.

BANFF SPRINGS HOTEL

One of the great attractions of the Banff Springs Hotel is its golf course (open to the public as well as to guests). Built with prisoner-of-war labour during World War I, it was redesigned in 1927.

The most prominent human landmark in the Rockies is the Banff Springs Hotel. When new in 1888, it was the world's largest hotel at 250 rooms. Back then, a day's stay cost $3.50. The Canadian Pacific Railway replaced the original building with a new one, constructed in the Scottish baronial tradition, between 1910 and 1928. Today it pampers its guests with superlative service, a spa, good restaurants, interesting shops, and outstanding sports facilities.

The Bow River and its famous falls run through the town of Banff. It flows 645 kilometres from the glacial waters of Bow Lake eastward to the Oldman River. A great way to experience the Bow is on a guided rafting trip.

*T*he Upper Hot Springs and Pool, fed by the naturally-heated springs of Sulphur Mountain, have attracted tourists since 1886. At forty degrees Celsius, they provide a nice hot soak for aching limbs.

SULPHUR MOUNTAIN GONDOLA

Sulphur Mountain gets its name from the smell of the hot springs near its base. At 2451 metres, this is a popular peak with visitors because it is easily accessible by gondola. The lift, built in 1959, is one of several in Banff National Park.

It whisks people to an elevation of 2285 metres in eight minutes inside roomy, safe, and glass-enclosed gondolas.

On top, visitors can stroll along a boardwalk to savour the mountain top and admire the

stunning views of the Bow River Valley, Lake Minnewanka, and neighbouring mountains. Hungry tourists can even enjoy a meal in the restaurant at the summit.
Brown bighorn sheep live on the mountain and often pester travellers in hopes of receiving tasty handouts. However, feeding them is not allowed, and visitors are advised to keep some distance between themselves and these 125-kilogram creatures.

LAKE MINNEWANKA

Today, Lake Minnewanka is larger than it was historically because the outlet of the original lake was dammed in 1912. In 1941 it was enlarged further. Now, it is twenty-five metres higher than it was before damming.

Lake Minnewanka is the largest body of water in Banff. Its peculiar name comes from the Cree expression for 'lake of the water spirit.' Today the lake boasts several recreational opportunities. Fishing is popular, and a tour boat allows travellers to enjoy its magnificent sights. Scuba divers enjoy visiting the former tourist resort of Minnewanka Landing, submerged in the early twentieth century when the lake was enlarged.

JOHNSTON CANYON

There are two ways to travel north from the Banff town site to Lake Louise: the Trans-Canada Highway and the Bow Valley Parkway. The latter is the more relaxed and scenic route. One popular stop along this road is the beautiful Johnson Canyon, located twenty-five kilometres north of Banff. The canyon is accessible along good walkways and catwalks that take visitors past seven dramatic waterfalls, including the stunning thirty-metre upper falls. Along the way tourists can see a grouping of six interesting springs, the 'Inkpots,' coloured a deep aqua by glacial sediments, as well as admire the rugged rock formations and beauty of the Canadian forest world while breathing in the fresh mountain air.

CASTLE MOUNTAIN

Castle Mountain, between Banff and Lake Louise, is a glorious hunk of limestone, dolomite, and shale that looms over the Bow River like a giant fortress. Popular with climbers, it rises to a height of 2766 metres above sea level.

*T*he high peaks are home for the golden and bald eagles. Bald eagles nest on tree tops while golden eagles prefer cliff edges, from which these great birds fly down in search of fish and small animals.

VERMILION LAKES

The Vermilion Lakes are an extensive region of montane wetlands near the Banff town site. Their name comes from the ochre beds at the iron-rich mineral springs at the Vermilion River pass where aboriginal people used to obtain materials

for some of their ceremonial body paints. The lakes are dominated by one of the most famous mountains in the Rockies, Mount Rundle. This imposing 2949-metre peak got its name in 1859 to honour Robert Rundle, a Methodist missionary who worked among the native population. The Canadian Rockies themselves start at the southern end of British Columbia and Alberta and extend north 1200 kilometres to the Liard River Basin near the Yukon.

LAKE LOUISE AND VICTORIA GLACIER

*L*ake Louise attracts visitors all year round. Warm-weather travellers can rent canoes at the
boathouse or savour countless breathtaking vistas along seventy kilometres of hiking trails.
In winter, ice sculptures, skiing, and snowshoeing delight cold weather enthusiasts.

Fifty-five kilometres north of the town of Banff are two of Canada's most famous natural attractions: Lake Louise and Victoria Glacier. Lake Louise is the daughter of Victoria Glacier. In the distant past, the glacier covered the whole lake.

It gradually deposited debris to form a landscape feature called a 'terminal moraine' which acted as a dam to hold meltwater as the glacier slowly retreated. Today the ninety-metre-deep lake is 2.4 kilometres long and five hundred metres wide.

CHATEAU LAKE LOUISE AND ...

The Chateau Lake Louise is one of Canada's best loved places to stay. It had its founding in the late nineteenth century for travellers who took the Canadian Pacific Railway west to enjoy alpine adventures. Ever on the lookout to improve the tourist trade, the railway added such creature comforts as electricity in 1916-17. Today, the chateau offers restaurants, a spa, shopping, and a variety of other fine amenities to keep its guests happy.

... OLD RAIL STATION

C oyotes are one of the Rockies' noted carnivores. These animal typically hunt at night, and capture their prey either by themselves or in pairs. They can run up to sixty kilometres per hour, which makes them formidable hunters.

The old railway station at Lake Louise served travellers for about a century until train service to the village came to a halt in the 1980s. Now, this historic building has become a bar and restaurant. It is just one of a number of facilities in Lake Louise dedicated to making tourists comfortable. Things were not always so pleasant: in 1884, the first tourist to Lake Louise found himself having to share his bed with a smelly drunk in a log shack!

MORAINE LAKE

About fifteen kilometres from Lake Louise is Moraine Lake in the Valley of the Wenkchemna Mountains. Many visitors feel that it is even more exquisite and spectacular than its more famous cousin.
The lake is misnamed! Walter Wilcox christened it in 1899, thinking that it had been created behind a glacial moraine – a kind of natural dam created by the debris left behind by a retreating glacier. However, the lake formed after a rock fall dammed the run-off from the surrounding mountains.

PEYTO LAKE

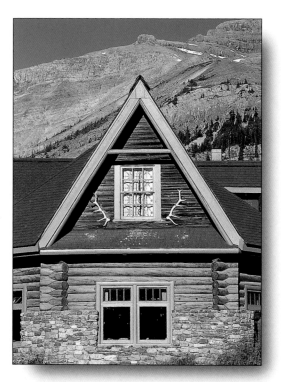

Located near the North Saskatchewan River drainage region, along Alberta's Icefields Parkway, travellers encounter Peyto Lake, celebrated for its natural beauty and turquoise water. The lake got its name from a famous guide and park warden, 'Wild Bud' Peyto, who came to the Rockies in the 1890s. Near the lake is the Num-Ti-Jah Lodge, a local landmark built in 1920 by Jimmy Simpson and his wife, Billy, who earned their living serving the needs of rich big-game hunters.

'Wild Bill' Peyto, after whom this beautiful lake is named, was an Englishman. Upon his arrival in the 1890s, he embraced the Rocky Mountain life and was noted for wearing fringed buckskins and for sporting a six-shooter on his hip.

MISTAYA CANYON

*G*rizzly bears are the larger of the two bear species found in the Rockies. These giants of the forest can be distinguished from the more common black bear by their large humps behind their shoulders.

43

Mistaya Canyon, located near the Icefields Parkway near the Saskatchewan River Crossing, developed over many centuries as the Mistaya River carved through the local limestone to form the valley. The river, like so many in the region, starts off in a glacier above Peyto Lake. At the canyon, visitors can enjoy a 1.5-kilometre trail that is easy enough for people to traverse in an hour. The word 'Mistaya' by the way, is a Stoney native expression for 'much wind.'

GLACIER NATIONAL PARK

C aribou (right) eat lichens, shrubs, roots, grasses, and mushrooms. Below: the monument to the Rogers Pass, discovered in 1881, which allowed the transcontinental railway to make its way through the Rockies.

Located along the Trans-Canada Highway, Glacier National Park in British Columbia is home to over four hundred glaciers amidst some of the tallest peaks in the Columbia Mountain Range. This range is situated west of the Rockies and is older, being composed of much harder rock. Therefore, its peaks are much sharper than those of the Rockies. The park presents wonderful opportunities to hike through the distinct ecological zones that make up its 1345 square kilometres of land.

YOHO NATIONAL PARK

Yoho is a Cree word meaning 'awe,' a fitting name for this enormous park with its many dazzling sights. Located in British Columbia, between Glacier and Banff national parks, it is home of the famous Takakkaw Falls. At 380 metres, these are Canada's second-highest waterfalls. ('Takakkaw' comes from the Stoney expression 'it is wonderful.') Another fascinating attraction in Yoho is the Burgess Shale Deposit with its extremely important collection of rare fossils dating back 530 million years.

FLORA

The Rockies are home to a tremendous variety of flowers and plants. There are four typical ecological zones in the region: the montane forest, the sub-alpine forest, the alpine tundra, and looming over all, the frozen mountain tops. The lower regions of montane forest contain various trees, the dominant ones being Douglas fir, white spruce, lodgepole, limber pine, trembling aspen, and balsam fir. Above this region is the sub-alpine forest, the home of spruce, sub-alpine fir, Lyall's larch, and white-bark pine trees.
(The Larch is particularly interesting, being a coniferous tree that loses its needles in the

autumn.) Above is the area of alpine tundra, a region marked by its magnificent flowers which prosper in these dry, windswept regions.
The Rockies are an astonishing place for the flower and plant enthusiast, being home to 996 different vascular plants (trees, grasses, and flowers) to say nothing of the dozens of lichens and other species.

CANOEING, FISHING, RIDING

The Rockies, are the place for the quiet outdoors enthusiast. Canoeing opportunities abound, whether one wants to head off into the wilderness or simply rent a canoe for a short paddle around a small lake. Fishing, of course,

The tea house at Emerald Lake in Yoho National Park is just one of many places to relax after an active day of canoeing, fishing, or riding.

49

flourishes in the Rockies. Visitors either can set out by themselves or hire guides to show them their favourite spots. Likewise, different outfitters take tourists on trail rides through the amazing beauty of the outback to see hidden parts of the Rockies that most travellers miss. Whether by canoe or in the saddle, these are wonderful opportunities to relive the lives of the early settlers when horses and canoes were the primary means of transportation in the region.

KOOTENAY
NATIONAL PARK

*T*he hot springs above in Kootenay Park
calm the souls and sooth the muscles of
today's visitors. Like their modern counterparts,
ancient people also enjoyed the hot springs, as
we know from their pictographs
found in the area.
The Kootenay River Valley, right, is a sublime
place to escape, unwind, and breathe fresh air.

Kootenay National Park lies south of Yoho National Park in British Columbia. It encompasses two river valleys, the Kootenay and the Vermilion, amidst the magnificent environment of the west side of the Rocky Mountains. Local wildlife use the Kootenay River Valley as a transportation corridor, and hence it offers excellent opportunities to see mule and white-tail deer, elk, black bear, coyotes, moose, and wolves. The Radium Hot Springs serve as

the park's major tourist destination. Situated in a picturesque setting below the cliffs of Sinclair Canyon, they consist of two outdoor pools. One is kept at a hot forty degrees Celsius for relaxation and the other is a cooler twenty-nine-degree swimming pool. Unlike other hot spring in the Rockies, these are virtually odourless, and possess only a small mineral content. However, as their name suggests, they do contain a tiny, but safe, amount of radiation.

SINCLAIR CANYON

Sinclair Canyon lies at the west end of Kootenay National Park.
In it visitors can see the kind of faults that allow steam and water to rise from inside the earth's crust to feed the neighbouring Radium Springs. In Kootenay, steam rises from a point 2414 metres below ground, condenses to water, and emerges at surface level at between thirty-two and fifty-four degrees Celsius.

MARBLE CANYON

Towards the north end of Kootenay Park is Marble Canyon, one of the most beautiful canyons in the park with its myriad plants, thirty-six metre cliffs, and stunningly-blue glacial meltwater. Visitors can enjoy a short hike through the forest to see the more scenic areas of the canyon. One highlight is the crossing at Tokumm Creek while another is the dramatic waterfall at the end of the trail.

*T*he rugged limestone cliffs of Marble
Canyon in Kootenay National Park
contrast with the rich green forest environment
and rushing blue waters of Tokumm Creek.   55
The name 'Tokumm' comes from the Stoney
people, and means 'red fox.' Nearby ochre beds
supplied the natives with red clay for
body paint.

*B*ighorn sheep travel in separate male and female herds except during the mating season. When mating, the rams crash their horns against each other in their contest for ewes. These sheep are extremely agile as they jump around treacherous mountain ledges, and they possess outstanding senses of smell, hearing, and sight.

KANANASKIS COUNTRY

Southeast of Canmore, Alberta lies the four-thousand-square-kilometre Kananaskis Country. It comprises the often overlooked front ranges of the Rocky Mountains, situated west of Calgary and south of Banff.

Kananaskis is the home of several ecological zones, including rolling foothills in the east, a higher montane region, alpine meadows, and farther west, an alpine zone at elevations of 1830 to 2440 metres, complete with glaciers

along the Continental Divide. One attraction of the region is the weather: it is generally warmer here than in the more famous national parks. As well, tourist crowds tend to be smaller. For western enthusiasts, this is the place to go for ranching vacations and trail rides. Skiing also is popular here, as are golfing, hiking, mountain climbing, horseback riding, fishing, camping, and a wide variety of other winter and summer sports.

ALPINE ADVENTURES

The Rocky Mountains offer some of the best slopes for the downhill skier to be had anywhere. In fact, the region's outstanding facilities were the home of the skiing events in the 1988 Calgary Olympics. In one region alone, the slopes of

59

Nakiska in Kananaskis Country, every conceivable skiing opportunity is available, from cross-country, to Olympic-quality downhill, to wild and dangerous heli-skiing, to the more recent craze of snowboarding.

*T*he moody weather encountered along the Trans-Canada Highway is typical of the Rocky Mountains. Many tourists come to Canada expecting it to be always cold. In summer, however, it can be downright hot. Yet, because of the elevations, Rocky Mountain weather can be fickle. One day it might be thirty degrees Celsius, the next, it might snow!

TRANS-CANADA HIGHWAY

The 7821-kilometre Trans-Canada Highway extends from the Atlantic to the Pacific. It is the favourite route for travellers in the Rockies, although sometimes it can be crowded because of the popularity of the mountains with tourists.

The Columbia Icefields, 105 kilometres south of the Jasper town site, cover 390 square kilometres of territory, sometimes to a depth of 365 metres! The best way to see them is on special vehicles that travel right onto the ice from the Icefields Centre.

JASPER NATIONAL PARK

Jasper National Park, established in 1907, is named after Jasper Howse, a local fur trader from the early nineteenth century. The centre of the park is the Jasper town site on the Athabasca River. Tourists began to arrive here shortly after the park became accessible via the Grand Trunk Pacific and Great Northern railways in 1911-12. In 1927, an all-weather road opened to Edmonton, 260 kilometres to the east. Today, Jasper is the largest national park in the Rockies at 10,880 square kilometres. It encompasses spectacular glaciers, lakes, rivers, canyons, forests, alpine tundra, and mountains. Amenities for travellers include the Miette Hot Springs, and a nice selection of restaurants, craft studios, and two small museums in the town itself, along a terrific range of warm and cold weather outdoor recreational and sightseeing opportunities.

TRAMWAY

*T*he Jasper Tramway is a glass-enclosed gondola that whisks people to the top of Whistlers Mountain at an altitude of 2277 metres. Absolutely glorious views are to be enjoyed from the summit, and on a clear day Mount Robson can be seen eighty kilometres away in British Columbia. The tramway is just one of Jasper's attractions that allow visitors to explore the natural and cultural history of the region.

ATHABASCA FALLS

A popular destination thirty kilometres south of the Jasper town site is the Athabasca Falls. Here, the Athabasca River is funnelled into a narrow canyon cut into the sandstone. The result: the twenty-five metre waterfall is among the most powerful in the Rockies.

MOUNT EDITH CAVELL

The majestic 3363-metre Mount Edith Cavell got its name in 1916 to honour a British Red Cross nurse who worked in a Belgian hospital. She was shot by the Germans after she helped allied prisoners escape. Nearby are the popular Angel and Cavell glaciers.

67

*O*ne of the best ways of enjoying Pyramid Mountain and the other attractions in Jasper is on a guided hiking tour, which can be booked in the Jasper town site. Both park staff and private operators offer guiding services to meet different interests and abilities.

PYRAMID MOUNTAIN

At 2766 metres, Pyramid Mountain dominates the local environment. Because of its height, there are no trees near the summit. There is too little soil and the growing season is too short up there to support large plants.

PYRAMID LAKE

Pyramid Lake, eight kilometres from the Jasper town site, is a glacial lake where visitors can fish or boat in its waters, or picnic, hike, or horseback ride around its shores. It also is one of only three lakes in the Rockies where motor boats can be used. Accordingly, water skiing is popular there.

PATRICIA LAKE

*P atricia Lake was the scene of one of the weirder
scientific projects of World War II. Canada and
its allies experimented with building a new kind of
unsinkable ship here, made out of ice and wood chips!
The experiment didn't work.*

Forty-metre-deep Patricia Lake is named
after Lady Patricia Ramsay, one of Queen
Victoria's granddaughters.
At the lake, tourists can rent a canoe and,
if they have a permit, can fish for rainbow trout.
There is a good trail around the lake
through jackpine, Douglas Pine, and aspen
woodlands for walking
and horseback riding.

*W*olves and cougars are two of the great hunters of the Rockies. Both possess powerful teeth, enormous strength, and are capable of chasing down their prey at considerable speeds. Wolves often hunts in packs, while cougars seeks their quarry by themselves.

ATHABASCA VALLEY

The Athabasca River is one of Canada's great waterways. Its historical importance was recognized in 1989 when the 168 kilometres of the river that run through Jasper were designated a Canadian Heritage River. The Yellowhead Pass in the Athabasca

Valley connects Jasper to Mount Robson Provincial Park across the Continental Divide. The pass is the lowest in the Rockies, and so was thought to be a possible route to reach the Pacific Ocean for Canada's transcontinental railway. However, engineers in the 1880s found it too difficult for the Canadian Pacific Railway and abandoned it as a route to the coast. About thirty years later the Grand Trunk Pacific, with more advanced technology, was able to cut its way through the pass.

MALIGNE CANYON

Rushing white water, sheer limestone rock faces, and dramatic wilderness scenery combine to make Maligne Canyon a spectacular place to visit. The canyon's drama can be explored along a good interpretive trail.

MALIGNE LAKE

Maligne Lake, at twenty-two kilometres long, is the largest body of water in the Rockies. The lake can be explored either in a rented canoe or boat, or on a larger tour boat.

76

Maligne Canyon, eleven kilometres from the Jasper town site, is not to be missed. It formed over ten thousand years as water and frost cut through the rock to a depth of fifty-five metres, although at some points it is barely a metre wide.

*C*lockwise from the lower left: grizzly or brown bear, moose, wild ducks, Canadian lynx, coyote, tawny owl, grey wolves – just some of the many creatures that find their homes in the Rocky Mountains.

FAUNA

The Rockies are home to a stunning variety of animals, both large and small, from majestic grizzly bears to incredibly cute chipmunks. Thus nature lovers from around the world descend on the region to commune with the animal kingdom.
Some creatures, such as black bears and elk, can be spotted with considerable ease. In fact, huge elk waltz right through the heart of downtown Banff! Others, such as cougars, are extremely reclusive. These cats hunt alone in the back country in search of prey, their favourite being mule deer.
Two other wild cats in the Rockies, also infrequently seen, are bobcats and lynx. Feathered hunters, which are more likely to appear to tourists, include eagles and ospreys. Eagles are the more common of the two. These huge creatures, with their two-metre wingspans, feed on fish, rabbits, rodents, and the dead animals they find.

81

83

Mount Robson Provincial Park sits inside British Columbia just west of Jasper National Park. Founded in 1913, it is the home of snow-capped mountains, deep canyons, icefields, lakes, and the upper reaches of the mighty Fraser River. Named after Mount Robson, the tallest peak in the Canadian Rockies at 3954 metres, the park has attracted mountain climbers for generations. Mount Robson itself probably was first conquered in 1911.

MOUNT ROBSON
PROVINCIAL PARK

WATERTON LAKES NATIONAL PARK

W Waterton Lakes National Park, an out-of-the-way scenic gem on the border with Montana beside the U.S. Glacier National Park, is not to be overlooked. Central to the park are the magnificent Waterton Lakes, the deepest in the Rockies at 150 metres, formed during the last ice age, eleven thousand years ago.

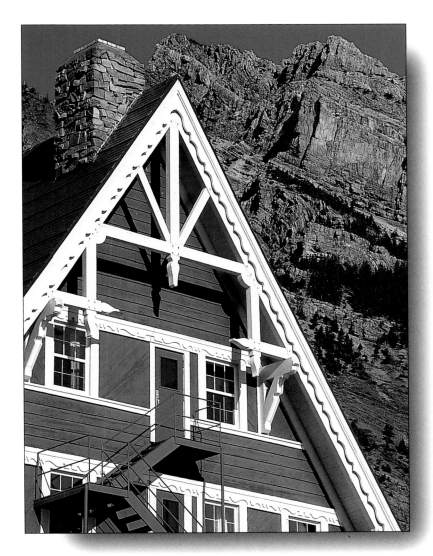

V isitors to Waterton often stay at the Prince of Wales Hotel, opened in 1927. Today the seven storey 'chalet' overlooking Waterton Lake (and named after the man who abdicated the throne in 1936 for Wallis Simpson) is open from mid-May to mid-September.

CAMERON FALLS

CAMERON LAKE

B oating joins wind surfing, hiking, cycling, and horseback riding, as a popular pastime at Waterton Lakes National Park.

Cameron Falls in the village of Waterton Park is a postcard-pretty waterfall that rushes over some of the oldest bedrock in the Rockies. Cameron Lake sits a short distance from the community, in a 'cirque,' a huge cut in the landscape created when glaciers dug a chunk out of the neighbouring mountains thousands of years ago. These are just two of the many beautiful attractions in this isolated park in southern Alberta.

89

RED ROCK CANYON

Visitors to Red Rock Canyon in Waterton Lakes National Park are amazed at the lurid reds and greens of the local argillite. While enjoying the sights, however, visitors need to keep a wary eye out for bears!

INDEX

Distributor:

Canadian Souvenir Sales Ltd.
Golden Eagle Building, Highway 93/95
Tel. (250) 347 9628
Fax: (250) 347 9011
Box 99, Radium Hot Springs
British Columbia
Canada V0A 1M0

Project and editorial conception: Casa Editrice Bonechi
Publication Manager: Monica Bonechi
Picture research: Fiorella Cipolletta
Cover and Graphic design: Fiorella Cipolletta
Make-up: Manuela Ranfagni
Editing: Patrizia Fabbri
Map: Stefano Benini - Firenze

Text: Carl Benn

Printed in Italy by Centro Stampa Editoriale Bonechi.

Photographs from archives of Casa Editrice Bonechi taken by
Andrea Pistolesi.

Photographs by courtesy of Canadian Souvenir Sales Ltd.:
*pages 25 below, 33 below, 43 below, 45, 56, 73, 80, 81 by Giuliano Cappelli; pages 46/47, 47 by Shawn Macneil;
pages 31, 58, 59 by Timothy G.M. Reynolds.*

ISBN 88-476-0717-5

*   *   *